What Are Literature Pockets?

In *Literature Pockets—Tall Tales*, nine imaginative tall tales come alive through fun, exciting projects. The activities for each story are stored in a labeled pocket made from construction paper. (See directions below.) Add the charming cover and fasten the pockets together to make a personalized Tall Tales book for each student to enjoy.

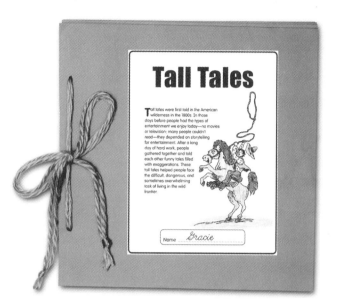

How to Make the Pockets

1. Use a 12" x 18" (30.5 x 45.5 cm) piece of construction paper for each pocket. Fold up 6" (15 cm) to make a 12" (30.5 cm) square.
2. Staple the right side of the pocket closed.
3. Punch two or three holes in the left side of the pocket.

How to Make the Cover

1. Reproduce the cover illustration on page 3 for each student.
2. Have students color and cut out the illustration and glue it onto a 12" (30.5 cm) square piece of construction paper to make the cover.
3. Punch two or three holes in the left side of the cover.
4. Fasten the cover and the pockets together. You might use string, ribbon, twine, raffia, or metal rings.

Step 1

Assemble a blank pocket book for each student. (See page 1.)

Step 2

Choose the first story you want to study. Reproduce the pocket label/bookmark page for students. Have students color and cut out the label and glue it onto the first pocket in their book.

Step 3

Complete the pocket.

• Have students color and cut out the bookmark and glue it onto a 4½" x 12" (11.5 x 30.5 cm) strip of construction paper. Have them use the bookmark to preview the story character.

• Reproduce the story for students and read it together. Students may track the text with the edge of their bookmark.

• Have students do the follow-up activities and place the paperwork in the pocket with their bookmark and story.

Tall Tales

Tall tales were first told in the American wilderness in the 1800s. In those days before people had the types of entertainment we enjoy today—no movies or television; many people couldn't read—they depended on storytelling for entertainment. After a long day of hard work, people gathered together and told each other funny tales filled with exaggerations. These tall tales helped people face the difficult, dangerous, and sometimes overwhelming task of living in the wild frontier.

Name _____

Pecos Bill

Pocket Label and Bookmark..........page 5
Have students use these reproducibles to make the Pecos Bill pocket label and bookmark. (See page 2.)

A Tall Tale About Pecos Bill......pages 6–8
Share and discuss this tall tale about Pecos Bill growing up in the wild with a pack of coyotes. Reproduce the story on pages 7 and 8 for students. Use the teaching ideas on page 6 to preview, read, and review the story. Follow up with the "More to Explore" activities.

Why Is It a Tall Tale?.....................page 9
Students express their understanding of tall tales by citing exaggerations and unbelievable details from the story. Work with students to complete this form.

Howling at the Moon.......pages 10 and 11
Students explore the art of perspective and lighting when they create a silhouette picture of Pecos Bill and his coyote family howling at the moon.

What Does It Mean?.......pages 12 and 13
This tall tale is filled with unusual words and phrases. Students create a little dictionary defining the terms.

Pecos Bill

Pecos Bill was a legendary cowboy invented by author Edward O'Reilly in *Century Magazine* in 1923. According to the many stories and movies that have been written about this superhuman cowboy since that time, he is strong enough, brave enough, and smart enough to rope a tornado and take care of all the cattle in Texas.

The fictional Pecos Bill grew up in Texas. His parents lost him out of their covered wagon near the Pecos River. He was raised by a pack of coyotes and didn't discover he was a human until he was a teenager.

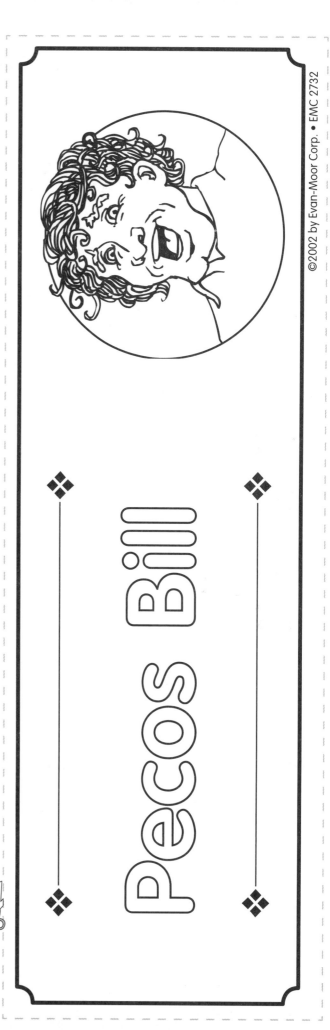

Share a Tall Tale About Pecos Bill

Preview the Story

Read and review the information on the bookmark with students. Then distribute copies of the tall tale (pages 7 and 8). Have students read the title and preview the pictures. Invite volunteers to predict what happens to young Pecos Bill.

Read the Story

Choose the most appropriate way for students to read the story—independently, with a partner, as a class, or following along as you read it aloud. Have students pause periodically to predict what happens next. During group reading or after independent reading, discuss any unfamiliar words, such as *fretted*, *ruckus*, *carted*, *varmints*, *burrs*, and *bared*. Point out context clues and picture clues that help explain the meanings of those words. After the discussion, have students reread the story to reinforce both comprehension and fluency.

Review the Story

Discuss the characters, setting, and plot of the story. Ask questions such as the following to help students recall important details, draw conclusions, and share opinions:

- How was Bill lost?
- Why do you think Old Coyote decided to raise Bill?
- What did Bill learn from Old Coyote?
- How did Bill discover that he was human?
- Why might getting "civilized" be a frightening prospect for someone raised in the wild?
- What do you think happened when Bill reached town?
- How do you know this story is a tall tale?

More to Explore

- The Old West

  Discuss the author's use of dialect. Explain to students that the way a character speaks can indicate when and where a story takes place. Have students find words and phrases in the story that indicate that it takes place in the "Old West."

- Old Coyote and the Lost Baby

  In this story, the coyotes have a meeting to decide what to do with Bill. Old Coyote convinces the pack to let him keep Bill. Have students write a paragraph telling what Old Coyote says to the other coyotes.

- More Tall Tales About Pecos Bill

  Have students use printed or online resources to find more tall tales about Pecos Bill. Invite volunteers to read the stories aloud. Ask students to identify the exaggerations and to compare the different versions of each tale.

How Pecos Bill Found Out He Was Human

Bill was the youngest of eleven children. Their thousand-acre farm was too small for all those kids, so Bill's family headed across Texas to find more farmland. There was a lot of singing, whistling, and pushing in the covered wagon. No one noticed when Baby Bill bounced out. His family didn't know he was missing until they stopped that night and counted noses.

Bill's mama fretted a lot about losing Bill, but she knew he'd find a way to get along. He could outcrawl, outholler, and outsmart all of his brothers and sisters.

As for Bill, he played in the Pecos River for a while. He got hungry about sunset and set up a terrible wailing. Old Coyote heard the ruckus and went to check it out. Bill looked interesting, so Old Coyote picked him up by his trousers and carted him off to a cave. He gave Bill some bones to chew, and that kept the young'n quiet until he fell asleep.

The coyotes had a meeting to decide what to do with Bill. He crawled around on four legs like the rest of them, but he didn't look like any coyote they'd ever seen. Old Coyote said Bill was his, since he found him, and he'd adopt him into the pack. He'd train him to be the best coyote around. None of the coyotes dared argue with Old Coyote, so he got his way.

Bill took to being a coyote. He learned how to sniff out a rabbit and howl at the moon. Old Coyote told him that the worst animals anywhere around were humans. "Skunks, snakes, and other varmints go about their own business, but humans," Old Coyote explained, "always interfere with everyone else's goings on."

Bill found he could run faster on two legs than on four, but the coyotes didn't pay him no mind. They were right fond of Bill even though he looked peculiar. He could take the burrs and stickers out of their fur better than any other coyote.

Bill stayed with the coyotes until he was fourteen years old. One day he came across a terrible odor. It was worse than a skunk and made the hair on his head stand up like spines on a cactus. A horse and another creature riding it were coming toward him.

"Must be one of them humans," Bill thought. "I'll take him on and get him out of coyote territory." Bill sat on all fours, howled, and bared his teeth. The human kept coming.

"You lost out here?" the human asked. "Lose your clothes? You're acting mighty strange. Sun get to you? I didn't know there were any humans out here."

Bill growled. "I'm a coyote!" snapped Bill.

"Coyote? You got no bushy tail," laughed the man. "You're human!"

Bill looked at his backside. He didn't have a tail. "I got fleas like coyotes."

"I got fleas too. That don't prove nothin'. Just look at yourself in that waterhole."

Bill looked at his reflection and the human's. How humiliating! He *was* a human!

"Come to the ranch and get civilized if you ain't afraid," said the human.

Bill wasn't afraid of anything—not even getting civilized. He howled farewell to the coyotes and loped off with the human.

Name: _____

Why Is It a Tall Tale?
Pecos Bill

Attributes of a tall tale:	How the attribute was used in this story:
larger-than-life main character	
problem solved in a funny way	
exaggerated details	

Pecos Bill

Howling at the Moon

Materials

- page 11, reproduced for each student
- 9" x 12" (23 x 30.5 cm) dark blue construction paper
- 6" (15 cm) square of yellow construction paper
- 6" x 9" (15 x 23 cm) black construction paper
- 1½" x 12" (4 x 30.5 cm) brown construction paper
- scissors
- glue
- white or yellow crayon
- writing paper

Steps to Follow

❶ Guide students through these steps to create a silhouette picture:

a. Round the corners of the yellow paper to make a large full moon. Glue the moon near the top center of the dark blue paper. Cut stars from the yellow scraps and glue them in the "sky."

b. Cut off an irregular strip along one long side of the brown paper to make the ground. Glue this along the bottom of the blue paper.

c. Cut out the templates of Pecos Bill and the coyotes. Place them on the black paper and trace around them with a white or yellow crayon. Cut out Bill and the coyotes, and glue them into the picture to show them howling at the moon.

❷ Have students write about howling coyotes. Give them a choice of these topics: write a fictitious tale about why coyotes howl at the moon, write a tall tale about Pecos Bill and the coyotes howling at the moon, or make a Fact v. Fiction chart and write about coyotes. Have students glue the paper onto the back of the picture.

Pecos Bill

Silhouettes

What Does It Mean?

Materials
- page 13, reproduced for each student
- scissors
- glue

Steps to Follow

❶ Ask students to look through the story to find the words and phrases listed below. Discuss each term. Point out context clues that help explain their meanings.

> fretted
> ruckus
> holler
> varmints
> pay him no mind
> right fond of
> carted him off

❷ Have students use the reproduced sheet to create a miniature dictionary of the words and phrases, as follows:

a. Cut and fold the sheet as marked.

b. Write a definition for each word and phrase in the folded dictionary.

❸ After students complete their dictionaries, have them write original sentences that include those words and phrases. Invite more advanced students to write a new adventure for Pecos Bill that includes some or all of the terms.

Pecos Bill

8

(writing lines)

carted him off

7

right fond of

(writing lines)

1

What Does It Mean?

by _____

6

pay him no mind

(writing lines)

2

(writing lines)

fretted

5

varmints

(writing lines)

3

(writing lines)

ruckus

4

holler

(writing lines)

fold 1 · fold 2 · fold 3 · cut

Slue-Foot Sue

Pocket Label and Bookmark........... page 15
Have students use these reproducibles to make the Slue-Foot Sue pocket label and bookmark. (See page 2.)

**A Tall Tale About
Slue-Foot Sue............................pages 16–18**
Share and discuss this tall tale about Slue-Foot Sue and her sweetheart Pecos Bill. Reproduce the story on pages 17 and 18 for students. Use the teaching ideas on page 16 to preview, read, and review the story. Follow up with the "More to Explore" activities.

Why Is It a Tall Tale?....................... page 19
Students express their understanding of tall tales by citing exaggerations and unbelievable details from the story. Work with students to complete this form.

A Folder Diorama .... pages 20 and 21
Students will get a kick out of making this pop-up diorama of Slue-Foot Sue bouncing on her bustle after being thrown by Widow Maker.

**More Than She
Could Chew ....pages 22 and 23**
Students explore the humor of idioms as they create their own illustrated minibook.

**The Slue-Foot
Sue Show.......................... pages 24 and 25**
This activity gives students the opportunity to "televise" the antics of Slue-Foot Sue. Students create a pull-through picture strip and write a script to go with it.

Slue-Foot Sue

Slue-Foot Sue was the oversized, legendary sweetheart of Pecos Bill. It was love at first sight when Bill saw her riding a whale-sized catfish down the Rio Grande. Sue was the perfect match for Bill. She was as stubborn as he was, and she could outrope and outride all of the cowboys on Pecos Bill's ranch, including Pecos Bill himself.

Slue-Foot Sue

Share a Tall Tale About Slue-Foot Sue

Preview the Story

Read and review the information on the bookmark with students. Then distribute copies of the tall tale (pages 17 and 18). Have students read the title and preview the pictures. Invite volunteers to predict how Slue-Foot Sue impresses Pecos Bill.

Read the Story

Choose the most appropriate way for students to read the story—independently, with a partner, as a class, or following along as you read it aloud. Have students pause periodically to predict what happens next. During group reading or after independent reading, discuss any unfamiliar words, such as *steer*, *lasso*, *ambled*, *tuckered*, *cowpokes*, and *bustle*. Point out context clues and picture clues that help explain the meanings of those words. After the discussion, have students reread the story to reinforce both comprehension and fluency.

Review the Story

Discuss the characters, setting, and plot of the story. Ask questions such as the following to help students recall important details, identify character traits, draw conclusions, and identify cause-and-effect relationships:

- Why did Slue-Foot Sue lasso Mr. Slippery Fins?
- What made Pecos Bill fall head-over-heels in love with Slue-Foot Sue?
- What reasons did Slue-Foot Sue give for agreeing to marry Pecos Bill?
- How did Slue-Foot Sue react to her wedding present? Why?
- What problem was caused by Sue's bustle? How was the problem solved?
- How would you describe Slue-Foot Sue?
- How do you know that this story is a tall tale?

More to Explore

- What Does It Mean?

  Have students write definitions and original sentences for these words from the story: *collard greens*, *spurs*, *lasso*, *rodeo*, *yonder*, *preacher*, *widow*, and *bustle*. Encourage them to look back in the story for context clues. If needed, have them look up the words in a dictionary. You may decide to have students make a mini-dictionary of the terms, as they did for the Pecos Bill pocket. (See page 12.)

- Dear Diary

  Have students write diary entries about what happened to Slue-Foot Sue. Students may write from Sue's or Bill's point of view. Remind them to use descriptive language and to express the emotions and feelings of the character. Encourage them to follow the style of writing used in the story.

- More Tall Tales About Slue-Foot Sue

  Have students use printed or online resources to find more tall tales about Slue-Foot Sue. Invite volunteers to read the stories aloud. Ask students to identify the exaggerations and to compare the different versions of each tale.

Slue-Foot Sue Meets Pecos Bill

Slue-Foot Sue had a dozen older brothers. They taught her how to ride wild horses, rope a steer, climb trees, wrestle grizzly bears, and make apple pie. Sue was a fine cook. She made a mess of collard greens, biscuits, and beans for herself and her brothers every evening.

One day Sue saw a catfish the size of a whale jumping around in the Rio Grande. "Where you going in such a hurry, Mr. Slippery Fins?" Sue yelled.

Well, the catfish didn't think it was any of Sue's business, so he kept on leaping around.

Sue thought that was mighty rude, so she threw her lasso in the air. She made it spin so fast it became invisible. When the catfish jumped higher than the trees, Sue roped him in and decided to take a ride. That catfish bucked like a bull in a rodeo, but Sue hung on. He dunked her in the water, but Sue didn't give up.

About that time Pecos Bill and his horse, Widow Maker, ambled along. Bill was so surprised to see Sue riding a catfish that he fell off his horse and head-over-heels in love. Sue was the prettiest gal he'd ever seen.

When the catfish tuckered out, Sue slipped off the rope and swam to shore. Right then and there Bill asked her to marry him. He didn't want her to get away.

"You're mighty handsome," Sue said. "Ain't nobody asked me to marry him before. I reckon I might. That's a good-looking horse you have. I guess you'd let your wife ride him."

 Literature Pockets—Tall Tales • EMC 2732

"I'd be glad to find you a horse, but not Widow Maker. I'm the only one who can ride him. Anyway, if you tell me your name and where you live, I'll bring the preacher by tomorrow."

"Name's Slue-Foot Sue, and I live over yonder," she answered.

"I'll be there about noon," Bill said.

The next day, Bill and the preacher were right on time. All the brothers were there. Bill brought a horse for Sue and a dozen cowpokes to be the best men.

After the wedding, while everyone was shoveling down the food, Sue sneaked outside to see her horse. It was right beside Widow Maker, and it was the tamest pony she'd ever seen.

"Won't do," thought Sue. Her wedding gown had a bustle that was bigger than a barn, but that didn't matter. She climbed up on Widow Maker and dug in her spurs. Widow Maker leaped around until he bucked her off. It didn't hurt, because Sue landed on her bustle. That bustle tossed Sue up in the air. Up and down she bounced, all the time hollering for help.

Bill and her brothers came running. "Like I said," Bill called to her, "nobody but Pecos Bill rides Widow Maker!"

Bill got out his rope and lassoed his bride in time to keep her from knocking a hole in the sun.

I can't say Slue-Foot Sue and Pecos Bill lived happily ever after, because Sue was always biting off more than she could chew. But after her wedding day, she did stay away from Widow Maker whenever she was wearing a bustle.

 Literature Pockets—Tall Tales • EMC 2732

Name: _____

Why Is It a Tall Tale?
Slue-Foot Sue

Attributes of a tall tale:	How the attribute was used in this story:
larger-than-life main character	
problem solved in a funny way	
exaggerated details	

A Folder Diorama

Materials
- page 21, reproduced for students
- a file folder for each student
- scraps of colored construction paper, including yellow, green, brown, and white
- crayons, colored pencils, marking pens
- scissors
- glue
- large paper clips
- long pipe cleaners
- clear tape
- large note cards

Steps to Follow

Guide students through the following steps to make a folder diorama:

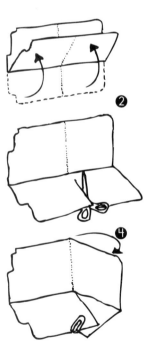

❶ Color and cut out the pictures of Slue-Foot Sue and Widow Maker on page 21. Glue them onto scraps of construction paper. Let them dry while you complete Steps 2, 3, and 4.

❷ Open the file folder and refold it horizontally. Cut along the original fold line to the center as shown.

❸ Color the top sections of the folder blue to represent the sky. Color the bottom sections brown to represent the ground.

❹ Overlap the cut sections to form the base of the diorama, as shown. Clip them together with a large paper clip.

❺ Cut out Slue-Foot Sue and Widow Maker from the construction paper. Fold under the flap on Widow Maker and glue it onto the diorama. Curl the pipe cleaner around a pencil to make a "spring." Tape Slue-Foot Sue to one end of the spring. Tape the other end of the spring to the diorama.

❻ Cut a sun from yellow construction paper and glue it onto the background. Make bushes, trees, and cactuses from green and brown construction paper. Fold under the bottom of each plant and glue it onto the diorama. Use paper scraps and marking pens to add other details to complete the scene.

❼ Write an explanation of the scene on a note card. Tape or glue the card onto the back of the diorama.

Note: To store the diorama in the pocket, remove the paper clip and carefully fold down Widow Maker and the plants. Press down Slue-Foot Sue and her spring. Fold the diorama. Use the paper clip to hold it shut.

Slue-Foot Sue

fold

More Than She Could Chew

Materials

- page 23, one or two copies reproduced for each student
- 4" x 5" (10 x 13 cm) pieces of construction paper
- colored pencils, marking pens
- scissors
- hole punch
- small metal rings or 6" (15 cm) pieces of yarn

Steps to Follow

❶ Use the expression "biting off more than she could chew" to introduce or review idioms with the class. Have students find the idiom in the last paragraph of the story. Point out that its literal meaning is not the same as the intended meaning.

❷ Work with students to list at least eight other idioms. Write the idioms on the chalkboard, and then discuss the meaning of each one. For example:

He *got up on the wrong side of the bed.*	You're *pulling my leg.*
She *has something up her sleeve.*	He *caught a cold.*
We'd better *stick together.*	She *got cold feet.*
She has a *green thumb.*	Someone *let the cat out of the bag.*
He *jumped down my throat.*	Stop *beating around the bush.*

❸ Have students use the reproduced sheets to make a minibook of idioms. For each page, have them write a sentence that includes an idiom, underline the idiom, draw a humorous picture of its literal meaning, and then write what it really means.

❹ Have students decorate two 4" x 5" (10 x 13 cm) pieces of construction paper to make the front and back cover of the book. On the front of the book, have them write the title "A Little Book of Idioms by _____," using their name to fill in the blank.

❺ As students decorate the cover and cut apart the book pages, pass around the hole punch for them to use. Have them put the book together, punch a hole in the top left corner, and then fasten it with a metal ring or a piece of yarn.

Slue-Foot Sue

More Than She Could Chew

Idiom: _____

_____

What it really means: _____

_____

_____

Idiom: _____

_____

What it really means: _____

_____

_____

Idiom: _____

_____

What it really means: _____

_____

_____

Idiom: _____

_____

What it really means: _____

_____

_____

The Slue-Foot Sue Show

Materials

- page 25, reproduced for students
- 6" x 9" (10 x 20 cm) construction paper
- 4" x 18" (7.5 x 45.5 cm) construction paper
- rulers
- Exacto® knives (adult supervision required)
- clear tape
- colored pencils
- scissors
- glue

Steps to Follow

❶ Guide students through these steps to create a pull-through "television" picture strip:

a. To make a television frame, cut two 3" (7.5 cm) horizontal slits in the 4" x 8" (10 x 20 cm) construction paper as shown. Cut the slits about ½" (1.3 cm) from the edges and about 3" (7.5 cm) apart. Then fold the paper in half and tape the edges together. (You may choose to cut the slits ahead of time for students or have them use scissors instead of an Exacto® knife to cut the slits.)

b. Use colored pencils to add details to the television set.

c. Cut out the six squares from the Television Strip sheet. Glue the squares onto the long construction paper strip, beginning with the title.

d. Choose five important actions from the story, and illustrate them in separate squares in correct sequence.

e. Slip the finished paper strip into the television frame. Pull it through to show what happened when Slue-Foot Sue met Pecos Bill.

❷ Have students write a script to go with their picture strip. Students may read the script aloud while a classmate pulls the strip through the television frame.

         Literature Pockets—Tall Tales • EMC 2732

Slue-Foot Sue

by _____

Slue-Foot Sue

by _____

Paul Bunyan

Pocket Label and Bookmark........page 27

Have students use these reproducibles to make the Paul Bunyan pocket label and bookmark. (See page 2.)

A Tall Tale About
Paul Bunyan ....pages 28–30

Share and discuss this tall tale about Paul Bunyan and his encounter with a swarm of unusual insects. Reproduce the story on pages 29 and 30 for students. Use the teaching ideas on page 28 to preview, read, and review the story. Follow up with the "More to Explore" activities.

Why Is It a Tall Tale?......................page 31

Students express their understanding of tall tales by citing exaggerations and unbelievable details from the story. Work with students to complete this form.

A Union of Insects................ pages 32–34

Students explore the union of the mosquitoes and the bees by writing a peace treaty and by drawing a labeled picture of their offspring.

A Book of Similes ....pages 35 and 36

Paul Bunyan was as tall as a mountain. His flapjack griddle was as big as a field. Starting with examples from the tall tale, students create their own book of similes.

Paul Bunyan

Paul Bunyan is a fictional giant who invented logging and all the tools to go with it. Early stories about Paul Bunyan were published in 1910 in the *Detroit News-Tribune*. More tales were written in advertising booklets for the Red River Lumber Company.

Paul Bunyan's imaginary adventures took place in logging areas in Michigan, Wisconsin, Minnesota, and other parts of the United States. According to tall tales, Paul logged off all the trees in North Dakota, dug out Puget Sound in the Northwest, and created the Grand Canyon and the Black Hills.

Paul Bunyan

Share a Tall Tale About Paul Bunyan

Preview the Story

Read and review the information on the bookmark with students. Then distribute copies of the tall tale (pages 29 and 30). Have students read the title and preview the pictures. Invite volunteers to predict the problems that Paul Bunyan solves.

Read the Story

Choose the most appropriate way for students to read the story—independently, with a partner, as a class, or following along as you read it aloud. Have students pause periodically to predict what happens next. During group reading or after independent reading, discuss any unfamiliar words, such as *harvest*, *logging*, *grinding wheel*, *conference*, and *griddle*. Point out context clues and picture clues that help explain the meanings of those words. After the discussion, have students reread the story to reinforce both comprehension and fluency.

Review the Story

Discuss the characters, setting, and plot of the story. Ask questions such as the following to help students recall important details, identify character traits, recall the sequence of events, and identify problems and solutions:

- What was unusual about Paul Bunyan? How was he different from other men?
- How did Paul and his lumberjacks help the farmers of North Dakota?
- How did Paul's inventions help make the lives of his lumberjacks easier?
- Why did Paul bring the bees to the logging camp?
- Where did the mosquitobees come from?
- How did Paul get rid of the mosquitobees?
- How do you know this story is a tall tale?

More to Explore

- Strange Insects

  Remind students that the double-stingered mosquitobees were a result of crossing a mosquito and a bee. Invite students to create new strange insects by combining two other insects. Have them draw their new insect and write a descriptive paragraph about its appearance and special skills.

- Continue the Tall Tale

  Have students continue the tall tale, telling what happened to the mosquitobees' parents and the other mosquitoes and bees at the logging camp. Conduct the activity as an oral storytelling, having students take turns adding on a sentence to the same tall tale, or have students work independently to write a new ending.

- More Tall Tales About Paul Bunyan

  Have students use printed or online resources to find more tall tales about Paul Bunyan. Invite volunteers to read the stories aloud. Ask students to identify the exaggerations and to compare the different versions of each tale.

Paul Bunyan

Paul Bunyan and the Giant Mosquitoes

Paul Bunyan towered over the trees in the forest. He was as tall as a mountain and could fell one hundred trees or more with one swing of his mighty ax. He made it look as easy as falling off a log!

Paul didn't feel it was fair to do all the work himself, as there were so many woodsmen who needed jobs. He hired a crew to help him harvest trees. It's a fact that he and his lumberjacks cleared all of the trees out of North Dakota so farmers had room to grow wheat.

Paul spent most of his time inventing new ways to make logging easier. One time his lumberjacks were too tired to climb over a mountain to the forest. So Paul hitched Babe, his giant blue ox, to the forest and hauled it to the logging camp.

Paul also saved the lumberjacks a lot of time and running around when he invented a grinding wheel to sharpen axes. Before Paul's wheel, the lumberjacks ran up and down hills, pulling their axes over rocks on the ground to sharpen them.

 Literature Pockets—Tall Tales • EMC 2732

Paul's grinding wheel worked fine until the attack of the giant mosquitoes. Before the mosquitoes went after the lumberjacks, they sharpened their stingers on Paul's grinding wheel. After an attack by the mosquitoes, the lumberjacks were as holey as pieces of Swiss cheese. Paul got tired of them putting holes in his men, so he imported some mosquito-eating bees.

It didn't help. The mosquitoes invited the bees to a peace conference. They passed around the peace pipe, and both the bees and the mosquitoes decided to work together. After the peace conference, some of the bees and the mosquitoes got married. Their offspring were double-stingered mosquitobees the size of eagles. They carried off some of the lumberjacks to their hives.

One day a whole swarm of mosquitobees went after Paul. He held a flapjack griddle that was as big as a football field over his head. The mosquitobees hit the griddle so hard that their stingers went right through it. They couldn't shake the griddle loose, so they buzzed off with it. The mosquitobees were tuckered out by the time they flew over Lake Michigan. They splashed into the lake and went underwater with the griddle. That was the last of them.

Paul Bunyan

Note: Reproduce this page for each student. Use the directions on page 26 to help students complete the activity.

Name: _____

Why Is It a Tall Tale?
Paul Bunyan

Attributes of a tall tale:	How the attribute was used in this story:
larger-than-life main character	
problem solved in a funny way	
exaggerated details	

Paul Bunyan

A Union of Insects

Materials

- pages 33 and 34, reproduced for each student
- scissors
- ribbon
- drawing paper
- crayons, colored pencils, marking pens

Steps to Follow—A Peace Treaty

❶ Discuss what might have occurred at the peace conference between the mosquitoes and the mosquito-eating bees. Have students consider what the two groups thought about each other and about Paul and his lumberjacks.

❷ Ask volunteers to explain the purpose of a peace treaty. Then have students brainstorm ideas for a peace treaty between the mosquitoes and the mosquito-eating bees. List their ideas on the chalkboard. You might consider having students role-play the negotiations between the two groups of insects.

❸ Have students use page 33 to write a peace treaty between the mosquitoes and the bees. Have them cut out the treaty, roll it up, and tie a narrow ribbon around it.

Steps to Follow—Mosquitobees

❶ Have students complete the Venn diagram (page 34), comparing and contrasting the characteristics of a mosquito and a bee. Have them consider both the physical features and the actions of both insects. Invite students to share what they wrote as you record their results in a large Venn diagram drawn on the board.

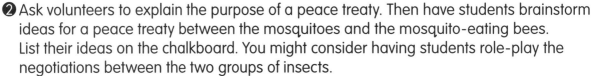

❷ Have students use what they learned to draw and label a picture of a mosquitobee on drawing paper. Remind them to include features of both a mosquito and a bee.

❸ Extend the activity by having students write a description to go with their picture. Have them identify the features of the insect and tell how those features might help the insect survive better than either of its parents.

Option

Invite students to create models of mosquitobees to display in the classroom. Provide a variety of building materials, such as plastic foam balls, modeling clay, pipe cleaners, toothpicks, clear plastic wrap, colored tissue paper, and paint.

Paul Bunyan

We, the undersigned, agree to

_____

_____

_____

_____

_____

_____

_____

_____

_____

_____

_____

Signed,

_____

_____

Literature Pockets—Tall Tales • EMC 2732

Name: _____

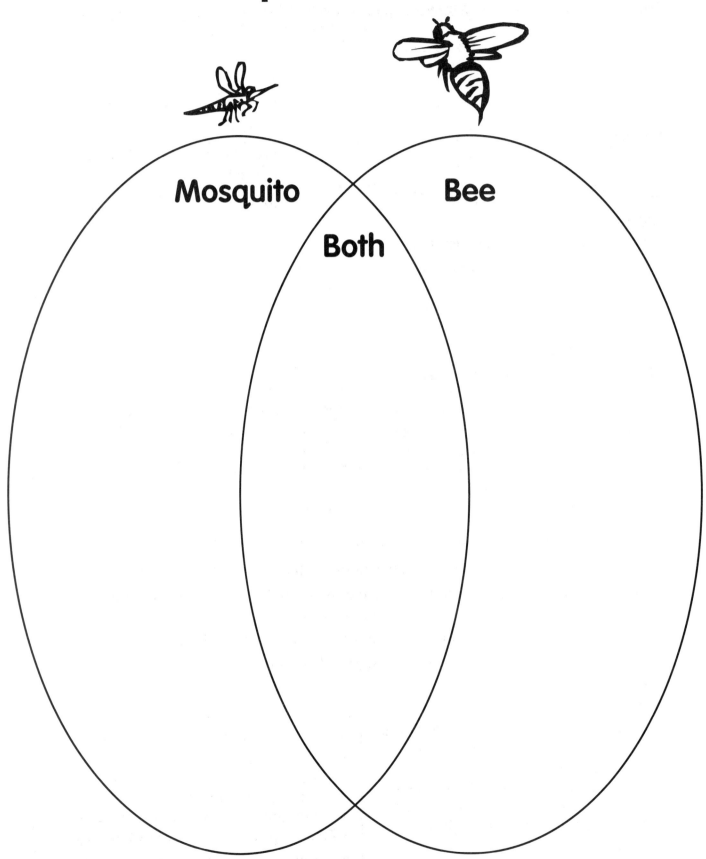

Mosquito

Bee

Both

A Book of Similes

Materials

- page 36, reproduced for each student
- 4" x 18" (10 x 45.5 cm) construction paper
- crayons, colored pencils, marking pens
- scissors
- glue
- white copy paper, ruler (optional)

Steps to Follow

❶ Explain to students that a simile is a figure of speech that compares two different things using the word *like* or *as*. Have students find the four similes in the story. Write the statements on the chalkboard, and ask students to identify the pairs of items being compared.

- He was as tall as a mountain.
- He made it look as easy as falling off a log.
- The lumberjacks were as holey as pieces of Swiss cheese.
- He held a flapjack griddle as big as a football field.

❷ Guide students through the following steps to make an accordion book of similes:

a. Accordion-fold the construction paper into six 3" (7.5 cm) sections as shown.

b. Complete the book forms by filling in the missing words and drawing a picture for each simile. On the last form, write your own simile and illustrate it.

c. Cut out the six forms and glue them onto the six front sections of the folded paper.

d. Refold the accordion book. Write "Similes" on the front outside cover.

Variation

Have more advanced students write similes about the people, places, things, and actions mentioned in the story. Have them cut and use six 3" x 4" (7.5 x 10 cm) pieces of white paper instead of the reproduced sheet. Share the examples at right if needed.

- Paul Bunyan worked as fast as a tornado.
- The lumberjack slept like a log.
- The buzzing bees were as loud as thunder.
- The mosquitoes were like flying syringes.
- The mosquitobees were as big as eagles.
- Paul Bunyan's wife was as sweet as sugar.

Paul Bunyan

A Book of Similes

is as _____

big as _____

1

is as _____

slow as _____

2

is as _____

long as _____

3

is as _____

soft as _____

4

is as _____

strong as _____

5

6

Literature Pockets—Tall Tales • EMC 2732

Babe the Blue Ox

Pocket Label and Bookmark........page 38
Have students use these reproducibles to make the Babe the Blue Ox pocket label and bookmark. (See page 2.)

A Tall Tale About Babe the Blue Ox.............................pages 39–41
Share and discuss this tall tale about a giant blue ox and his companion Paul Bunyan. Reproduce the story on pages 40 and 41 for students. Use the teaching ideas on page 39 to preview, read, and review the story. Follow up with the "More to Explore" activities.

Why Is It a Tall Tale?....................page 42
Students express their understanding of tall tales by citing exaggerations and unbelievable details from the story. Work with students to complete this form.

Big Babe...page 43
Using large sheets of butcher paper, students create a large portrait of Babe and then write descriptive phrases inside the huge character.

Saddlebags of Frozen Words........................pages 44–46
After making a pair of saddlebags, students fill them with equal amounts of "frozen words" that the lumberjacks might have said during the cold winter.

A Poem About Babe.......pages 47 and 48
Students review different forms of poetry and then use one of the forms to write a poem about Babe.

Babe the Blue Ox

Babe was an enormous, imaginary ox who worked alongside the giant logger, Paul Bunyan. He was so big that lumberjacks, standing near his tail, had to use spyglasses to see his head.

It's reported that Babe was white before the Winter of the Blue Snow. Standing in the blue snow for days changed his color.

Babe was the strongest animal invented by American storytellers. He could haul a whole forest of trees to the sawmill all by himself.

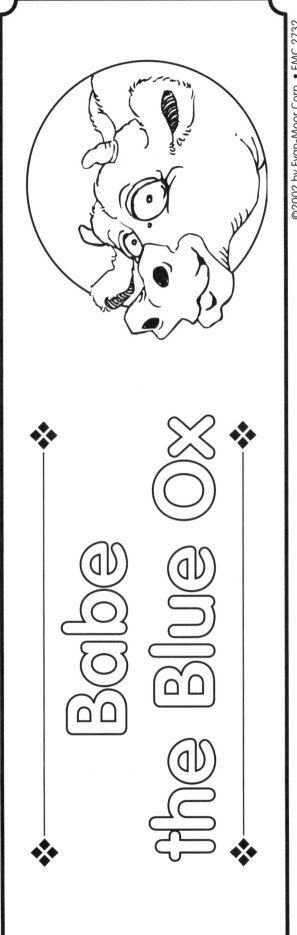

Babe the Blue Ox

Share a Tall Tale About Babe the Blue Ox

Preview the Story

Read and review the information on the bookmark with students. Then distribute copies of the tall tale (pages 40 and 41). Have students read the title and preview the pictures. Invite volunteers to predict how Babe helped Paul Bunyan.

Read the Story

Choose the most appropriate way for students to read the story—independently, with a partner, as a class, or following along as you read it aloud. Have students pause periodically to predict what happens next. During group reading or after independent reading, discuss any unfamiliar words, such as *snowdrifts*, *thawing*, *bunkhouse*, *saddlebags*, and *hitch*. Point out context clues and picture clues that help explain the meanings of those words. After the discussion, have students reread the story to reinforce both comprehension and fluency.

Review the Story

Discuss the characters, setting, and plot of the story. Ask questions such as the following to help students identify important details, recall the sequence of events, and identify cause-and-effect relationships:

- How did Babe and Paul get together?
- What was unusual about Babe's size and appearance?
- Why did Paul and Babe hike across North America? Where did they go next?
- How did Paul and Babe get white snow to their logging camp?
- Why did Babe dump the frozen words behind the trees instead of in a canyon?
- What caused the noisy ruckus in the springtime?
- Why did Babe leave Paul?
- How do you know this story is a tall tale?

More to Explore

- Compound Words

  Have students use the following list of words to form 10 compound words from the story. Point out that some of these words may be used more than once: *lumber, snow, bunk, red, saddle, after, some, country, flap, cook, noon, side, where, drifts, jacks, house, bags,* and *wood. (lumberjacks, snowdrifts, bunkhouse, redwood, saddlebags, afternoon, somewhere, countryside, flapjacks,* and *cookhouse).*

- How Many Flapjacks?

  Challenge students to solve the following math problem: If Paul ate a mile-high stack of flapjacks, and each flapjack was ½" high, how many flapjacks did he eat? *(126,720 flapjacks)* Then have students write and solve their own math problems about Babe and Paul.

- More Tall Tales About Babe the Blue Ox

  Have students use printed or online resources to find more tall tales about Babe the Blue Ox. Invite volunteers to read the stories aloud. Ask students to identify the exaggerations and to compare the different versions of each tale.

Paul Bunyan and Babe the Blue Ox

Some lumberjacks say that Babe didn't turn blue until the Winter of the Blue Snow. That may or may not be, but there's no doubt that Paul Bunyan found his giant ox under a pile of blue snowdrifts. Paul called him Babe because he was a baby. Paul thought Babe might turn brown or white after he pulled him out of the snow, but Babe stayed true blue all his life.

Babe soon grew bigger than the bunkhouse, and bigger than any barn. It was a good thing that the snow never bothered him because there wasn't a building big enough to cover him. He grew to be twenty-four axe handles wide between the eyes, and it took a crow a full day to fly from one horn to the other.

Babe's first adventure with Paul was during the Blue Snow, when Babe was just a few months old. Paul and his lumberjacks got tired of their clothes turning blue when they washed them in snow water. So Paul and Babe set off to see what they could do about it. They hiked across North America and didn't find any white snow at all. The Pacific Ocean was frozen over, so they made some wooden skates from giant redwood trees and skated over the ocean. Babe had a little trouble staying on his feet at first, but he got the hang of it before they reached China. The snow was white there, so Paul threw a bunch of snowballs across the ocean to his logging camp. Then he loaded Babe with snow, and they headed home. When they got back to the logging camp, Babe dumped the white snow over the blue.

 Literature Pockets—Tall Tales • EMC 2732

There were two winters that year. The snow kept coming and coming. It got so cold that all the lumberjacks' words froze as soon as the letters left their mouths. Lumberjacks were skidding and falling on their own words all over camp. Babe filled two giant saddlebags with frozen words. Paul told him to drop them in a canyon somewhere.

Babe was feeling lazy and cold after his trip to China, so he dumped the words behind the trees near the bunkhouse. One afternoon all those words thawed out. The ruckus from a winter's worth of words traveled all over the countryside. Babe tried to stomp out the noise, but it did no good. The words kept thawing out all spring. After that, the lumberjacks were mighty careful about what they said, and they remembered to say "please" and "thank you."

Babe continued to help Paul for many years. His favorite job was straightening crooked roads. Paul would hitch Babe to the end of a road, and Babe would pull and stomp until the road was as straight as Paul's suspenders. Babe wore out miles of chain and himself besides, but he knew there'd be a mile-high stack of flapjacks waiting for him in the cookhouse once he had the road in line.

When Paul took up farming, Babe tried plowing. He was always stepping on the apple trees and knocking over the barn. Farming didn't agree with Babe, so one day he headed toward Canada, and no one has seen him since. He's probably somewhere in the deep woods dreaming about flapjacks.

Babe the Blue Ox

Name: _____

Why Is It a Tall Tale?
Babe the Blue Ox

Attributes of a tall tale:	How the attribute was used in this story:
larger-than-life main character	
problem solved in a funny way	
exaggerated details	

Big Babe

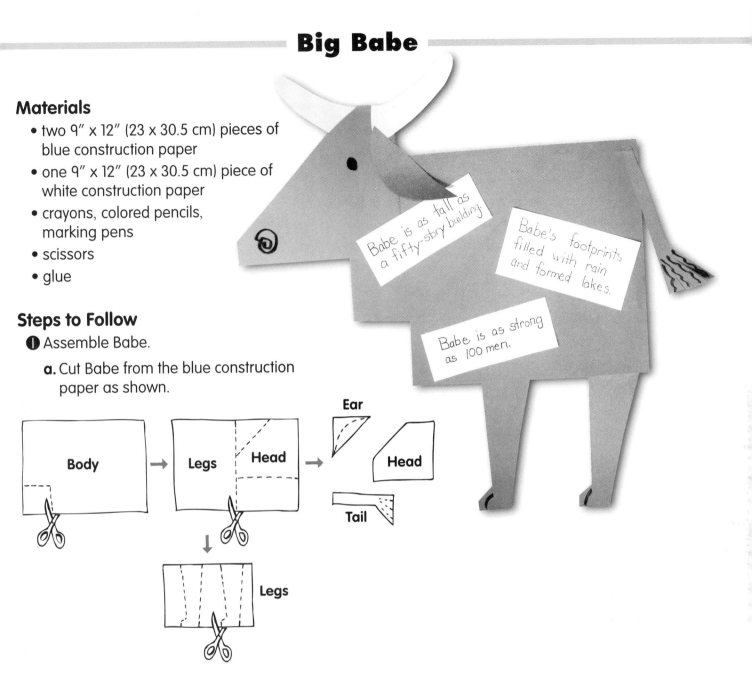

Materials

- two 9" x 12" (23 x 30.5 cm) pieces of blue construction paper
- one 9" x 12" (23 x 30.5 cm) piece of white construction paper
- crayons, colored pencils, marking pens
- scissors
- glue

Steps to Follow

❶ Assemble Babe.

a. Cut Babe from the blue construction paper as shown.

Body

Legs | Head

Ear

Head

Tail

Legs

b. Glue the sections together.

c. Cut horns from the white paper. Glue them in place.

❷ Write descriptive sentences about Babe on the leftover white paper. Cut out the sentences and paste them onto his body.

Babe is as tall as a fifty-story building.

Babe's footprints filled with rain and formed lakes.

Babe is as strong as 100 men.

Note: Have students fold Babe to fit him in the pocket.

Babe the Blue Ox

Saddlebags of Frozen Words

Materials

- pages 45 and 46, reproduced for each student
- 6″ x 9″ (15 x 23 cm) pieces cut from brown paper bags, three for each student
- brown and black crayons
- scissors
- staplers
- glue

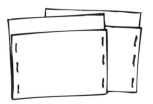

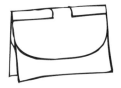

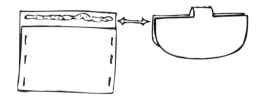

Steps to Follow

❶ Remind students that Babe filled his giant saddlebags with "frozen words." Then explain to students that they will be calculating the weight of frozen words and distributing them equally into two saddlebags.

❷ Guide students through the following steps to make a pair of saddlebags to hold the frozen words:

a. Wrinkle each piece of brown paper and then smooth it flat. Use the side of a brown or black crayon to lightly rub color over the paper to give it a leathery look.

b. Fold one piece of brown paper in half. Place the saddlebag template on the fold as indicated. Trace around the template. Cut along the lines (not along the fold) to make a pair of connected pouch flaps.

c. Use the remaining two pieces of paper to form the pouches. Fold up the bottom of each piece, leaving about 1″ (2.5 cm) of space. Staple the sides.

d. Glue the flaps onto the pouches as shown. Let them dry.

e. Finish the saddlebags by drawing an outline on each piece as shown.

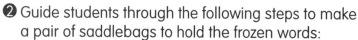

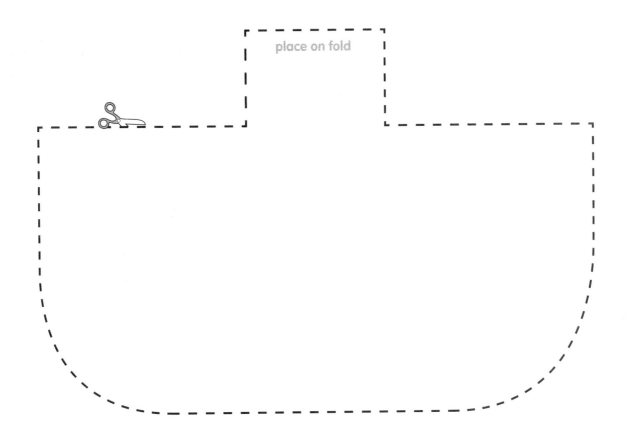

place on fold

❸ Have students cut out the words on page 46. Tell them that each frozen consonant weighs 2½ pounds, and each frozen vowel weighs 1½ pounds. Have them write the total weight of each word on the back of the cutout.

❹ Have students distribute the words equally between the two saddlebags so that each bag holds the same amount of weight. Have them write the total weight of each bag on the inside flap (total weight of each bag: 61½ pounds).

timber! (13 lb)	lumber (13 lb)	heavy (10½ lb)	tired (10½ lb)
cold (9 lb)	ouch! (8 lb)	freezing (17 lb)	
yikes! (10½ lb)	giant (10½ lb)	suppertime! (21 lb)	

❺ Extend the activity by having students add more story-related words to the saddlebags. Remind them to distribute the weight equally.

Babe the Blue Ox

Frozen Words

 timber!

 cold

 ouch!

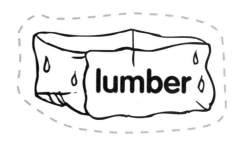 lumber

 tired

 yikes!

 freezing

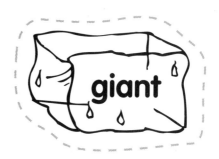 giant

 heavy

 suppertime!

A Poem About Babe

Materials

- page 48, reproduced for each student
- writing paper
- construction paper slightly larger than the writing paper
- crayons, colored pencils, marking pens

Steps to Follow

❶ Work with students to list possible topics for poems about Babe the Blue Ox. Write the suggestions on the chalkboard. For example:

Babe
Huge, powerful
Straightened crooked roads
Best friend to Paul
Ox

> a description of Babe's size and strength
>
> one of Babe's adventures written in rhyme
>
> a poem about Babe and his friendship with Paul Bunyan

❷ Give each student a copy of page 48. Review the steps for writing the various kinds of poems. Note: The cinquain form given is a simplified one. A cinquain poem may also consist of five lines of two, four, six, eight, and two syllables, respectively. You may choose to follow that format if you have writers who need a challenge. Here is an example of a cinquain that follows the formal pattern:

> Snowflakes
> Soft, cold, and wet
> Cool kisses of winter
> Float downward from the sky above
> Calmly

❸ Have students choose one of the poetic forms and write a poem about Babe. Students may select a topic from the board or think of a new idea. (You might consider having pairs of students work together.)

❹ Have students glue the poems onto construction paper to frame them. Students may draw a picture at the bottom of the poems or draw a decorative border around them.

Babe the Blue Ox

Guidelines for Writing Poems

A Couplet Poem: A short or long poem consisting of pairs of rhyming lines.

1. Think about the topic. Decide what you want to tell in your poem. Write your first line.
2. Make a list of words that rhyme with the last word of your first line.
3. Write your second line. It must have the same number of syllables as the first line and end with a rhyming word.
4. Write as many couplets as you need to share a complete, vivid poem.

Example:

I threw a snowball in the air.
It fell and landed in my hair.

A Cinquain Poem: A five-line verse consisting of one, two, three, four, and one word, respectively.

1. Write a one-word topic.
2. Write two words that describe the appearance of your topic.
3. Write a three-word phrase that describes an action or feeling about your topic.
4. Write a four-word phrase that describes an action or feeling about your topic.
5. Write one powerful word that refers to your topic.

Example:

Snow
Soft, cold
Kisses of winter
Drift from the sky
Breathtaking

An Acrostic Poem: The letters of a word are written vertically and used to begin each line of a poem about that word.

1. Choose a one-word topic. Write it down the page vertically.
2. Make a list of words or short phrases that describe or relate to the topic. The words must begin with a letter in the topic word.
3. Write the word or phrase after the correct letter, using that letter in the spelling.

Note: An acrostic poem may also be written so that the last letters of the lines spell a word. You may choose to follow that format.

Example:

Small flakes of frozen water
Not hard nor sharp
Open your mouth to catch some
Watch the flakes melt on your hand

Babe the Blue Ox

John Henry

Pocket Label and Bookmark ....page 50
Have students use these reproducibles to make the John Henry pocket label and bookmark. (See page 2.)

A Tall Tale About John Henry ....pages 51–53
Share and discuss this tall tale about how John Henry outdrilled a steam machine. Reproduce the story on pages 52 and 53 for students. Use the teaching ideas on page 51 to preview, read, and review the story. Follow up with the "More to Explore" activities.

Why Is It a Tall Tale? ....page 54
Students express their understanding of tall tales by citing exaggerations and unbelievable details from the story. Work with students to complete this form.

A Steel-driving Man ....pages 55 and 56
Just as John Henry was "a steel-driving man," students use a similar phrase to describe a talent or trait that they possess.

A John Henry Flip Book ....pages 57 and 58
Students make a flip book of a steel-driving man in action.

An Eyewitness Account.................page 59
Students write a newspaper article about the contest between John Henry and the steam machine.

John Henry

The legendary John Henry was a steel driver for the Chesapeake & Ohio Railroad. In songs and stories, John Henry died after outdrilling a steam drill at the Big Bend Tunnel in West Virginia in 1870.

Some of the tales about John Henry could have come from events in a real person's life, or from feats performed by many different people. No one is sure, but people who worked on the tracks at the same time the stories took place have claimed to know him.

Real or invented, John Henry is a hero for workers all over the United States.

Share a Tall Tale About John Henry

Preview the Story

Read and review the information on the bookmark with students. Then distribute copies of the tall tale (pages 52 and 53). Have students read the title and preview the picture. Invite volunteers to predict why John Henry is upset about a steam machine.

Read the Story

Choose the most appropriate way for students to read the story—independently, with a partner, as a class, or following along as you read it aloud. Have students pause periodically to predict what happens next. During group reading or after independent reading, discuss any unfamiliar words, such as *bales*, *ties*, *foreman*, *readied*, *ached*, and *chugged*. Point out context clues and picture clues that help explain the meanings of those words. After the discussion, have students reread the story to reinforce both comprehension and fluency.

Review the Story

Discuss the characters, setting, and plot of the story. Ask questions such as the following to help students recall important details, identify character traits, and draw conclusions:

- What jobs did John Henry do before he went to work for the railroad?
- Why was John Henry upset about the steam machine?
- What was the purpose of the contest?
- How did Polly Ann help John Henry during the contest?
- How would you describe John Henry's character?
- Why might John Henry be considered a hero?
- How do you know this story is a tall tale?

More to Explore

- By Hand or Machine?

  Discuss the advantages and disadvantages of doing tasks by hand versus machine. Have students list tasks they do each day that are better done by hand. Then have them draw and write about a machine they would invent to complete a certain task more efficiently.

- An Interview with John Henry

  Have pairs of students write and role-play an interview between a reporter and John Henry before the competition. Have them brainstorm questions to ask John Henry and then make up appropriate answers for the questions. Remind students that the questions and answers should relate to the story.

- More Tall Tales About John Henry

  Have students use printed or online resources to find more tall tales about John Henry. Invite volunteers to read the stories aloud. Ask students to identify the exaggerations and to compare the different versions of each tale.

John Henry

John Henry and the Steam Machine

John Henry went looking for work. He picked cotton and planted the fields. He rolled bales of cotton from the dock, up a plank, and into a ship. No matter what he did, he could outwork any man. That wasn't enough for John Henry.

"Polly Ann," he said to his wife, "there's only one job for me. I'm a steel-driving man. I've got to have a hammer in my hand."

Polly Ann knew there was no use arguing. She packed up, and they set off. Railroad companies were putting down tracks all over the country, and John Henry found the job he wanted.

All day long, John Henry lifted his twelve-pound hammer and drove steel spikes into the wooden ties that held the rails in place. He pounded ten hours a day, singing while he worked. John Henry moved so fast that his hammer heated up. The setters poured cool water over his hammer so it didn't start a fire.

John Henry heard that the Chesapeake & Ohio Railroad was building track through Big Bend Mountain. The C&O was hiring steel drivers to pound spikes into the rock. John Henry traveled to West Virginia and showed the foreman that he was the steel-driving man he needed.

After John Henry drove the spikes into the rock, the spikes were pulled up. Dynamite was stuffed into the holes and fired. Rock flew out of the middle of the mountain. When the hole was tunnel-sized, the C&O would set track for their trains.

All went well until a man with a steam drill told the foreman that his machine could outwork a steel-driving man any day.

"No steam machine is going to beat me down," John Henry said. "We'll have a contest, that machine and I. I'll die with my hammer before I'll let that mess of steel and steam win."

"Agreed," said the man with the machine. "We'll see who can pound the deepest holes, John Henry or my machine."

Now Polly Ann thought John Henry should just move on. There were enough rails to set between West Virginia and California to keep both machines and men busy. But she knew there wasn't any use saying it, so she fixed a mess of breakfast for John Henry and went to the mountain with him.

John Henry readied his hammer. The spike setters were in line. When the foreman gave the signal, John Henry started to pound at one end of the tunnel and the machine at the other.

After an hour, John Henry's muscles ached. Polly Ann could see he was tiring. She and the other women who had come to see the race sang. Polly kept the song going as fast as John Henry could swing a hammer. The machine was ahead of John Henry, but he didn't give up. Then the machine chugged its last blast of steam and broke down. John Henry kept pounding.

When the foreman gave the signal, men measured the holes. The ones pounded by the machine were half as deep as John Henry's. "No machine can beat John Henry," the foreman shouted. "He's the winner!"

John Henry didn't hear the cheers. He fell to the ground, his hammer in his hand. Polly Ann cradled his head in her lap. "You won, John Henry. You beat that machine."

"I knew I could," John Henry whispered. "No machine can outpound a real steel-driving man." He sighed and stopped breathing.

"John Henry died with his hammer," Polly sang to the crowd around them. "He died with the hammer in his hand. Oh, yes! John Henry was a steel-driving man."

John Henry

Name: _____

Why Is It a Tall Tale?
John Henry

Attributes of a tall tale:	How the attribute was used in this story:
larger-than-life main character	
problem solved in a funny way	
exaggerated details	

John Henry

A Steel-driving Man

Materials

- page 56, reproduced for each student
- crayons, colored pencils, marking pens
- glue
- 9" x 12" (23 x 30.5 cm) construction paper

Steps to Follow

❶ Ask students to explain why John Henry was called "a steel-driving man." Then explain that they are to think of a similar phrase that describes themselves. This may describe a talent or special trait they possess. For example:

> Anna is a book-reading girl.
> Arturo is a goal-scoring boy.
> Miyeko is a picture-painting girl.

❷ Say to students, "John Henry always had a hammer in his hand. The hammer was something a steel-driving man needed." Ask students to think of one thing (a book, a ball, etc.) that might be included in the drawing they make of themselves.

❸ Distribute the reproduced sheets for students to color. On the right side, have them draw a picture of themselves holding an object that reflects their talent. Below the picture, have them write the descriptive sentence about themselves.

❹ Have students glue the finished page onto construction paper to frame it.

Variation

Students might prefer drawing pictures of classmates rather than themselves. Give them the option of working with a partner and drawing each other's portrait.

John Henry

John Henry and Me

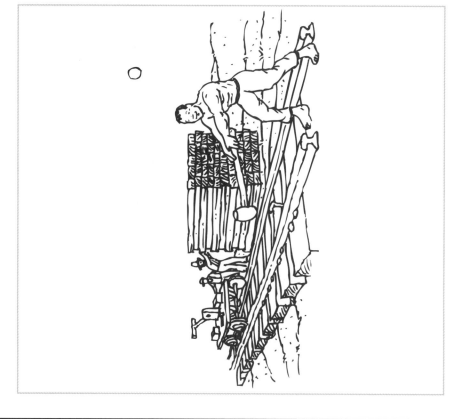

John Henry was a steel-driving man.

A John Henry Flip Book

Materials

- page 58, reproduced for each student
- scissors
- colored pencils
- stapler

Steps to Follow

Have students complete these steps to make a flip book of a steel-driving man:

❶ Cut out the flip book pages on page 58.

❷ Draw the ties and the spike on each page.

❸ Stack the pages in order and staple in the upper-left corner.

❹ Students flip through the finished pages to watch the figure hammer in the spike.

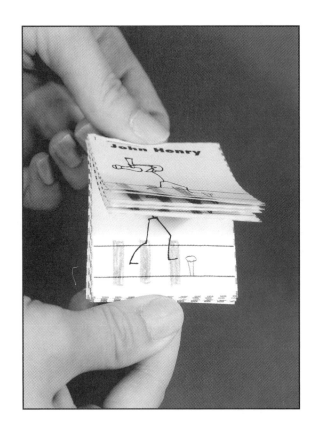

John Henry

Note: Reproduce this page for each student. Use the directions on page 49 to help students complete the activity.

Name: ____

An Eyewitness Account

headline

Davy Crockett

Pocket Label and Bookmark............. page 61

Have students use these reproducibles to make the Davy Crockett pocket label and bookmark. (See page 2.)

A Tall Tale
About Davy Crockett ....pages 62–64

Share and discuss this tall tale about Davy Crockett and his encounters with a raccoon and Halley's comet. Reproduce the story on pages 63 and 64 for students. Use the teaching ideas on page 62 to preview, read, and review the story. Follow up with the "More to Explore" activities.

Why Is It a Tall Tale?......................... page 65

Students express their understanding of tall tales by citing exaggerations and unbelievable details from the story. Work with students to complete this form.

Problems and Solutions .... page 66

Students draw and write about two problems that Davy Crockett solved. Their finished work should show these problems and solutions: 1) Because there was no moon to light up his way, Davy caught some fireflies in a lantern to use for light; 2) After Davy tried unsuccessfully to shoot down a comet headed for Earth, he grabbed the comet by the tail and flung it away from the planet.

Folded Paper Raccoon .... page 67

Students make an origami raccoon, and then write a story about the little rascal.

Halley's Comet .... pages 68 and 69

Students assemble a minibook of facts about Halley's comet, and then use that information to identify facts and fictitious details in the tall tale.

Davy Crockett

The real David Crockett was born in 1786 in Green County, Tennessee. He was a hunter and frontiersman who served under General Andrew Jackson and fought against American Indians.

He became a member of the Tennessee State Legislature and served in the United State Congress. He died fighting against Mexican soldiers at the Alamo in Texas.

Legends and tall tales about Davy Crockett came from a series of *Crockett Almanacs* that were written between 1838 and 1856. Storytellers have added to Crockett's impossible feats in the almanacs, and their legends about Davy Crockett grow bigger each time they are told.

Share a Tall Tale About Davy Crockett

Preview the Story

Read and review the information on the bookmark with students. Then distribute copies of the tall tale (pages 63 and 64). Have students read the title and preview the pictures. Invite volunteers to predict how Davy Crockett stopped a comet from crashing into Earth.

Read the Story

Choose the most appropriate way for students to read the story—independently, with a partner, as a class, or following along as you read it aloud. Have students pause periodically to predict what happens next. During group reading or after independent reading, discuss any unfamiliar words, such as *fireflies, budge, cabin, congress, comet,* and *wobbled.* Point out context clues and picture clues that help explain the meanings of those words. After the discussion, have students reread the story to reinforce both comprehension and fluency.

Review the Story

Discuss the characters, setting, and plot of the story. Ask questions such as the following to help students recall important details, draw conclusions, identify the sequence of events, and identify problems and solutions:

- What was unusual about Davy's hunting technique?
- Why wasn't Davy successful at grinning the raccoon out of the tree?
- Why do you think the members of Congress asked Davy for help?
- Why did Davy climb to the highest peak of the Rocky Mountains?
- What did Davy do about Halley's comet? What did he attempt to do before grabbing the comet's tail? Why didn't he use his secret weapon?
- How do you know this story is a tall tale?

More to Explore

- The Power of a Grin

  In this tall tale, Davy grinned all the bark off a tree. Have students consider the power of a real grin. Have them list ways that a grin could help solve problems.

- The Real Davy Crockett

  Have students conduct research to find out more about the real Davy Crockett. Have them create a Fact v. Fiction chart or make trivia cards about Davy Crockett to share with the class.

- More Tall Tales About Davy Crockett

  Have students use printed or online resources to find more tall tales about Davy Crockett. Invite volunteers to read the stories aloud. Ask students to identify the exaggerations and to compare the different versions of each tale.

Davy Crockett

Davy Crockett, Problem-solving Man

Davy Crockett went hunting in the forest one evening with the dog he called Bones. There wasn't any moon, so Davy caught some fireflies in a lantern so he could see where his feet were going. Davy noticed a big bump on a tree. "Looks like we got ourselves a raccoon," he said.

Now Davy didn't bother packing his gun around. He had a secret weapon, a skin-stretching, ear-to-ear grin. Not many people hunted with their grins, but it was all Davy needed.

"Stay back and close your eyes," he told Bones. "I'll grin that raccoon out of his tree."

Davy put two fingers in his mouth and stretched his grin a leg wide. He grinned right at the raccoon. After an hour or so, his mouth started to ache, but the raccoon didn't fall out of the tree like it should. Davy couldn't talk while he grinned, so he couldn't tell that raccoon to start falling. He just grinned wider. His grin pushed his ears to the back of his head, and they popped off.

That raccoon didn't budge. Nothing like this had happened before. Davy pushed his mouth back in place and wound on his ears. Then he went to his cabin for his ax. "I'll get you yet, Mr. Raccoon," he said, and he chopped down that tree.

When the tree fell, Davy was surprised to see that there wasn't any raccoon in that tree at all. He'd been grinning at a big knot on the trunk. Davy didn't feel so bad, because he'd grinned all the bark off the tree.

When people had problems they couldn't fix, they asked Davy for help. They even sent him to Congress. One time Halley's comet was heading right for old Mother Earth. The president of the United States and all the other people in Congress asked Davy to take care of the situation.

Davy headed for the Rocky Mountains and hiked to the highest peak he could find. He shouted at Halley. "No use heading this way. You'll make a mess of yourself if you crash around here!"

The bright comet kept coming. "It probably can't hear a thing with that long tail of sparks whipping around," Davy thought. "And there isn't any use trying to grin the comet away, because comets don't have eyes."

Davy tried to shoot Halley out of the sky, but the comet was so hot that the bullets melted before they hit their mark. Halley was getting closer all the time. When it was an arm's length away from Davy, he grabbed the comet's tail and spun that comet upside down and backwards. Halley tried to pull away and almost lost its tail. Davy kept whipping the comet around until Halley was so dizzy it just wobbled off into space. It took about 76 years before Halley was brave enough to get close to Earth again.

Davy Crockett

Name: _____

Why Is It a Tall Tale?
Davy Crockett

Attributes of a tall tale:	How the attribute was used in this story:
larger-than-life main character	
problem solved in a funny way	
exaggerated details	

Davy Crockett

Name: _____

Problems and Solutions

Directions: Explain what Davy Crockett's problems were and how he solved them.

Problem:

_____

_____

Solution:

_____

_____

_____

_____

_____

Problem:

_____

First Attempt to Solve the Problem:

_____

_____

Solution:

_____

_____

Davy Crockett

Note: Reproduce this page for each student. Use the directions on page 60 to help students complete the activity.

Folded Paper Raccoon

Materials

- 3" (7.5 cm) square of gray paper
- 7" (18 cm) square of gray paper
- black marking pen
- glue
- writing paper

Steps to Follow

❶ Fold the small square to make the head of the raccoon.

a.

b.
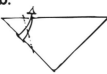

c.

d.

❷ Use a black marking pen to draw the face.

❸ Fold the large square to make the body.

a.
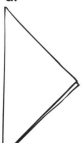

b.
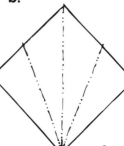

c.

d.

e.
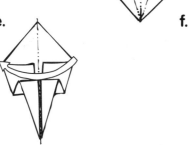

f.

g.

❹ Color the stripes on the tail. Glue the head to the body.

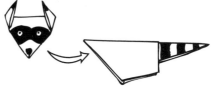

❺ After you finish making the raccoon, write a short story about how a raccoon outsmarted Davy Crockett. Mention Davy's "secret weapon." Glue the paper raccoon to your story.

Davy Crockett

Halley's Comet

Materials

- page 69, reproduced for each student
- crayons, colored pencils, marking pens
- scissors
- writing paper or copy paper
- 9" x 12" (23 x 30.5 cm) construction paper
- glue

Steps to Follow

❶ Have students color, cut out, and fold the reproduced sheet to make a minibook of facts about Halley's comet.

❷ Have students read the minibook and reread the tall tale to compare facts and details about Halley's comet. Have them make a Fact v. Fiction chart, using the minibook as a reference to help them decide which details from the tall tale are facts and which ones are fiction.

❸ Have students glue the chart onto construction paper to frame it. Students may add an illustrative border.

❹ To extend the activity, have students use printed or online resources to learn more about Halley's comet and other comets. Provide time for students to share what they discover.

Literature Pockets—Tall Tales • EMC 2732

Halley's comet was last seen in 1986. At that time, space probes took pictures of the comet. The photos showed that the comet's core is shaped like a potato and is surrounded by ice boulders and a cloud of gas and dust.

Facts About Halley's Comet

Halley's comet was named after its discoverer, Edmond Halley, who was the first person to prove that all comets orbit the sun. Edmond realized that this particular comet reappeared in the sky every 76 years. In 1682 he correctly predicted that it would return in 1758.

Like all comets, Halley's comet is made of ice, gas, and dust. The sun's heat causes the icy core to begin to melt, releasing long streams or "tails" of gas and dust that shine by reflecting sunlight.

Alfred Bullfrog Stormalong

Pocket Label and Bookmark ....page 71
Have students use these reproducibles to make the Alfred Bullfrog Stormalong pocket label and bookmark. (See page 2.)

A Tall Tale About
Alfred Bullfrog Stormalong ....pages 72–74
Share and discuss this tall tale about the misadventures of a giant seaman and his oversized ship. Reproduce the story on pages 73 and 74 for students. Use the teaching ideas on page 72 to preview, read, and review the story. Follow up with the "More to Explore" activities.

Why Is It a Tall Tale?...........................page 75
Students express their understanding of tall tales by citing exaggerations and unbelievable details from the story. Work with students to complete this form.

The *Colossus*.......................................page 76
Using drawing paper and the directions on page 76, students draw Stormalong's ship, the *Colossus*, and then write a description of the ship. Remind students to include vivid details and to use time-order words such as *first*, *next*, and *last* when writing the description.

A Map of the
Colossus's Routes ....pages 77 and 78
Students mark a map and write navigational directions to show and tell the routes that Stormalong followed at sea.

A Sailor's Journal..................pages 79 and 80
Students pretend to be sailors aboard the *Colossus* and write journal entries about the voyage.

Alfred Bullfrog Stormalong

Alfred Bullfrog Stormalong was a seafaring giant invented by storytellers who told tales about his nautical adventures. Stories agree that Stormalong came from an American town somewhere on the Atlantic Coast. He didn't stay anywhere very long because he outgrew every town, house, and ship there was.

Stormalong built his own oversized ship. It was so big that he hinged the mast tips so he could pull them down to let the moon go by.

Today, in Stormalong's honor, all sailors use the initials, A.B.S., after their names. If you ask, they say the initials stand for "able-bodied seaman."

Share a Tall Tale About Alfred Bullfrog Stormalong

Preview the Story

Read and review the information on the bookmark with students. Then distribute copies of the tall tale (pages 73 and 74). Have students read the title and preview the picture. Invite volunteers to predict what happens when Alfred sails his ship near England and Panama.

Read the Story

Choose the most appropriate way for students to read the story—independently, with a partner, as a class, or following along as you read it aloud. Have students pause periodically to predict what happens next. During group reading or after independent reading, discuss any unfamiliar words, such as *port, starboard, scaffold, hoisted, commotion, dinghy,* and *trench.* Point out context clues and picture clues that help explain the meanings of those words. After the discussion, have students reread the story to reinforce both comprehension and fluency.

Review the Story

Discuss the characters, setting, and plot of the story. Ask questions such as the following to help students recall important details, identify character traits, draw conclusions, and identify cause-and-effect relationships:

- How was Alfred Bullfrog Stormalong different from other sailors?
- Why did Alfred have to build the *Colossus*? Give at least three reasons.
- Why was *Colossus* a good name for Alfred's ship?
- According to this tall tale, how did the cliffs of the Strait of Dover become white?
- What fortunate accident happened when some sailors fell off the wheel while steering the *Colossus* near the Isthmus of Panama?
- How do you know this story is a tall tale?

More to Explore

- More Than One Meaning

  Several sailing-related words in the story also have other meanings. Have students write two definitions for each of the following words: *port, wheel, deck,* and *steer.* One definition must reflect the meaning in the story. Then ask students to write a sentence for each meaning.

- Able-bodied Seaman

  The bookmark tells us that Alfred Bullfrog Stormalong's initials stood for "able-bodied seaman." Ask students to use their own initials to write a phrase that describes themselves. For example: Alice Susan Fowler, A.S.F., A Super Friend!

- More Tall Tales About Alfred Bullfrog Stormalong

  Have students use printed or online resources to find more tall tales about Alfred Bullfrog Stormalong. Invite volunteers to read the stories aloud. Ask students to identify the exaggerations and to compare the different versions of each tale.

Alfred Bullfrog Stormalong

Alfred Bullfrog Stormalong
Sails the *Colossus*

Alfred Bullfrog Stormalong was the tallest and strongest sailor that ever lived. No ordinary sailing ship was big enough for him. Every time he stepped from the port to the starboard side of a ship, it rocked around like it was hit by a hurricane. Stormalong had to sleep on the deck because of his size. Several times he tipped over a ship when he rolled about in his sleep. The sailors complained about the splashing, but Stormalong always turned the ship right-side up before they fell into the water.

Stormalong solved the problem by building his own clipper ship that was bigger than the state of Massachusetts. He named his ship *Colossus*.

With a good wind, the *Colossus* crossed an ocean in record time. Even so, Stormalong liked to take shortcuts. Once he headed for the English Channel. He realized he'd miscalculated as soon as he saw the narrow passageway between England and France. The *Colossus* would tear open when it squeezed by the dark cliffs. Stormalong dropped anchor and rang the ship's bell. The sailors gathered around him. "Round up all the soap you can find," Stormalong bellowed. "Soap the sides of the ship until the suds are as thick as the blubber on a whale."

The crew hung scaffolds on the side of the ship and soaped the outside of the *Colossus*. After they used up every sliver of soap, Stormalong pulled the scaffolds back on board. He hoisted anchor and set sail for the Strait of Dover.

The *Colossus* creaked and groaned as it brushed against the dark cliffs. When the ship was in the open sea, Stormalong looked back. The cliffs were as white as the sails on his ship. The water bubbled up around the cliffs. "Looks like the *Colossus* did a good job cleaning up Dover," Stormalong said. So much soap rubbed off the *Colossus* that the cliffs are still white today.

The *Colossus* had another close call. Stormalong was headed for the islands in the Caribbean Sea. He decided to take a nap and let the crew take over. Stormalong had no trouble steering the *Colossus*. He could turn the great ship's wheel with his pinky. It took forty of his men hanging onto the wheel to keep the ship on course while he slept.

When the crew steered around an island, some of the men fell off the wheel. A blast of wind sent the *Colossus* dead ahead, and it plowed right through the Isthmus of Panama.

The commotion woke Stormalong, but it was too late. The *Colossus* was drifting across the Pacific Ocean. Stormalong turned the ship around, dropped anchor, and rowed a dinghy to shore. There was a bunch of men staring at the deep trench of water connecting the Atlantic Ocean to the Pacific.

Stormalong apologized and offered to fill the trench with dirt, but the men cheered. Stormalong couldn't figure out why they were so happy.

One of the men stepped forward. "The United States government sent us here to dig a canal so ships could pass from one ocean to the other. We've been digging for years. The *Colossus* finished the job. Now we can go home."

Stormalong sailed back through the canal and took the workers to the United States. They agreed not to mention the *Colossus*. They promised to tell the president that the canal was ready and their work was finished, which was the truth. If the president knew how easily the *Colossus* had dug that canal, Stormalong knew he would spend the rest of his days plowing canals with his ship.

Alfred Bullfrog
Stormalong

Name: _____

Why Is It a Tall Tale?
Alfred Bullfrog Stormalong

Attributes of a tall tale:	How the attribute was used in this story:
larger-than-life main character	
problem solved in a funny way	
exaggerated details	

Alfred Bullfrog Stormalong

The *Colossus*

Directions: Follow these instructions to draw a picture of the *Colossus* on drawing paper. Then write a description of the ship on the back of your picture.

A Map of the *Colossus's* Routes

Materials

- page 78, reproduced for each student
- overhead transparency of page 78
- overhead projector and markers
- crayons, colored pencils, marking pens

Steps to Follow

❶ Have students recall the places Alfred Bullfrog Stormalong and his crew sailed in the *Colossus*. Encourage them to refer back to the story.

❷ Use the overhead transparency to guide students as they draw the routes that the *Colossus* sailed through the Strait of Dover and the Panama Canal. Have students start from the same location along the Atlantic Coast, such as Boston, and then identify possible routes the ship could have traveled. Have them draw the shortest routes on the map. Students should mark the Dover route in one color and the Panama route in another. As students draw, have them say their course of direction (north, south, east, west) and identify places along the route.

❸ After students draw the routes, have them write navigational directions to go with the map.

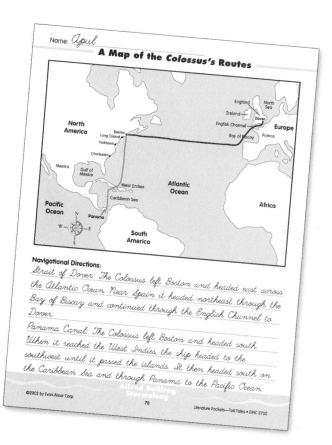

Alfred Bullfrog Stormalong

Name: _____

A Map of the *Colossus's* Routes

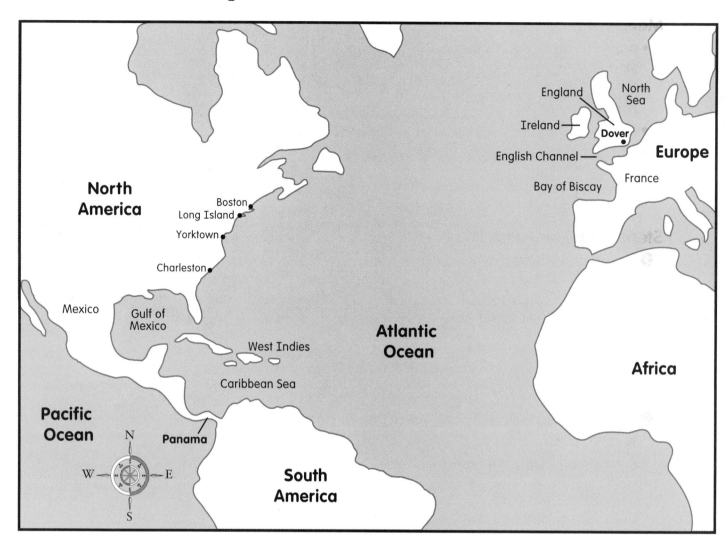

Navigational Directions:

_____

_____

_____

_____

_____

_____

_____

A Sailor's Journal

Materials

- page 80, two copies reproduced for each student
- 12" x 18" (30.5 x 45.5 cm) construction paper
- scissors
- glue
- crayons, colored pencils, marking pens

Steps to Follow—Journal

❶ Explain to students that they are to pretend to be a sailor sailing aboard the *Colossus* with Captain Stormalong. Their task is to record journal entries about events that occur during their travels. The entries should include descriptions of the events and the crew's reactions to those events.

❷ Guide students through the following steps to make a journal book:

a. Fold the construction paper as shown.

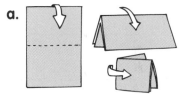

b. Open the paper and cut on the fold as shown, stopping at the horizontal fold.

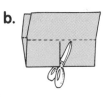

c. Fold in half lengthwise. Then push in the ends.

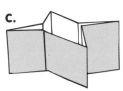

d. Cut apart the writing forms and glue one to each of the inside pages.

e. Write a title and draw a cover picture on the front of the book.

f. Complete the journal pages. Write a new entry on each page. Remember to date each entry and to include vivid details from a crewman's point of view.

Alfred Bullfrog Stormalong

_____
date

_____

_____

_____

_____

_____

_____

_____
date

_____

_____

_____

_____

_____

_____

_____
date

_____

_____

_____

_____

_____

_____
date

_____

_____

_____

_____

_____

_____

Mose the Firefighter

Pocket Label and Bookmark ....page 82

Have students use these reproducibles to make the Mose the Firefighter label pocket and bookmark. (See page 2.)

A Tall Tale About Mose the Firefighter ....pages 83–85

Share and discuss this tall tale about how Mose fought fires better than any other firefighter. Reproduce the story on pages 84 and 85 for students. Use the teaching ideas on page 83 to preview, read, and review the story. Follow up with the "More to Explore" activities.

Why Is It a Tall Tale? ....page 86

Students express their understanding of tall tales by citing exaggerations and unbelievable details from the story. Work with students to complete this form.

Mose Grows Up ....pages 87 and 88

Using pages that vary in size, students create a unique minibook that shows and tells information about Mose at different stages and sizes of his life.

A Proclamation of Honor ....page 89

Students complete a certificate describing Mose's heroic deeds and listing ways to honor him. Refer students to the deeds described in the story and help them brainstorm ways to honor Mose.

How to Put Out a Volcano ..... pages 90 and 91

Students use a volcano-shaped writing form to describe how Mose put out a fire in a volcano.

Mose
the Firefighter

The real-life model for Mose the Firefighter was Moses Humphries, a printer for a newspaper and a fireman on the Lady Washington, Engine No. 40, during the early 1800s. He, like the legendary Mose, fought fires and anyone who got in his way.

The tall tales about Mose, a city folk hero, grew from a series of New York plays about a rough-talking, kindhearted firefighter. On stage he rescued babies and ladies in distress. He was loyal to his firefighter companions, and eventually moved from New York to California. From there he sailed to the Sandwich Islands, which are now known as the Hawaiian Islands.

Mose
the Firefighter

Share a Tall Tale About Mose the Firefighter

Preview the Story

Read and review the information on the bookmark with students. Then distribute copies of the tall tale (pages 84 and 85). Have students read the title and preview the picture. Invite volunteers to predict how Mose helps New York City.

Read the Story

Choose the most appropriate way for students to read the story—independently, with a partner, as a class, or following along as you read it aloud. Have students pause periodically to predict what happens next. During group reading or after independent reading, discuss any unfamiliar words and phrases, such as *tenement house*, *water wagon*, and *man the hose*. Point out context clues and picture clues that help explain the meanings of those terms. After the discussion, have students reread the story to reinforce both comprehension and fluency.

Review the Story

Discuss the characters, setting, and plot of the story. Ask questions such as the following to help students recall the sequence of events, identify important details, identify problems and solutions, and share opinions:

- How did Mose end up being raised by Fire Company No. 40?
- What do you suppose happened to the other members of Mose's family?
- How did Mose's size and strength help him as a firefighter? Give examples.
- What problem happened in New York City when Mose was 21 years old? How did Mose solve the problem?
- Why did Mose leave New York City?
- How do you think the people of New York City felt about Mose? Why?
- How do you know this story is a tall tale?

More to Explore

- Character Web

  Have students create a character web about Mose the Firefighter. Have them list words and phrases that describe Mose's appearance, personality, and actions. Then have them write descriptive sentences about Mose.

- Then and Now

  Ask students to compare modern firefighting equipment and techniques with those in Mose's time. Work together to make a Venn diagram or a comparison chart. Encourage students to go online or search library resources to find more information.

- More Tall Tales About Mose the Firefighter

  Have students use printed or online resources to find more tall tales about Mose the Firefighter. Invite volunteers to read the stories aloud. Ask students to identify the exaggerations and to compare the different versions of each tale.

Mose the Firefighter

Mose, the Hero Firefighter

When Mose was three months old, he lived in a tenement house in New York City. The building where he lived caught fire, and Fire Company No. 40 rushed to the scene. The firefighters pulled the water wagon up to the building and found some tubs of water sitting in front of a laundry. They pumped the water as fast as they could, but by the time the first blast of water from their hose hit the flames, the building blew up. They couldn't save anyone. Boards and furniture flew into the air.

Firefighter Tony raised his hands and caught a cradle. When he looked inside, there was a baby, still asleep. Now the firefighters at Fire Company No. 40 were used to rescuing babies from burning buildings. It was their favorite job. But this time there were no grateful parents or aunts and uncles to claim the little fellow. The baby sat up and put Tony's fire hat on his head. Every man in Fire Company No. 40 cheered. They carried the baby back to the firehouse and named him Baby Mose.

Mose went to all the fires when he was growing up, and he grew up very fast. By the time he was two, he could fill a bucket with water and toss it to a firefighter. When he was five, he could man the hose. A few years later he pumped water.

All the fire companies in New York tried to get to a fire first. They raced along the streets pulling their wagons. When Mose was ten years old, Fire Company No. 40 won all the races. Mose was taller than a two-story house and twice as wide. He pulled the wagon by himself and hooked up the water before anyone else got to the scene. All the pigs and food carts cleared the streets when they heard Mose coming.

When Mose was twenty-one, the whole city of New York caught on fire. All the fire companies rushed to the scene, but they couldn't find enough water to put out the fires. Mose hooked every fire hose in the city together. They reached all the way to the Hudson River. He pumped the river water through the hose. The firefighters kept the water flowing all night and half of the next day.

Every drop of water was drained out of the Hudson River. The fish were flopping around the riverbed looking foolish, and the boats were stuck in the mud. River water was running through the streets of New York. People rowed around the city, and animals swam about looking for dry land.

Mose got right to work. He dug a tunnel from the river to the city, and came out on Fifth Avenue. The water flowed through the tunnel. Before the mayor could pin a medal on Mose for saving New York City, all the water was back in the Hudson.

Mose continued to help people in New York for many years. He did his share of baby-saving and rescuing beautiful ladies. He probably saved most of the people in New York at some time or another. He gathered up furniture and food for anyone who needed help after a fire. If he received a reward for rescuing someone, he shared it with the other firefighters at Fire Company No. 40.

When horse-drawn water wagons were invented, and there were enough fire hydrants in the city to supply water for the fire companies, Mose knew it was time to move along. He went to California to fight forest fires. After that he shipped out to the Sandwich Islands to put out fires in the volcanoes.

Name: _____

Why Is It a Tall Tale?
Mose the Firefighter

Attributes of a tall tale:	How the attribute was used in this story:
larger-than-life main character	
problem solved in a funny way	
exaggerated details	

Mose the Firefighter

Mose Grows Up

Materials

- page 88, reproduced for each student
- crayons, colored pencils, marking pens
- scissors
- glue

- 12" x 18" (30.5 x 45.5 cm) light blue construction paper
- writing paper (optional)

Steps to Follow

Guide students through the following steps to make an accordion-fold book about Mose:

❶ Color the pictures of Mose. Use picture clues and story information to fill in the correct ages. Then cut out the six rectangular sections.

❷ Fold the construction paper in sixths.

❸ Glue the title "Mose Grows Up" in the first section. Glue the pictures of Mose in order, one in each remaining section.

❹ In pencil, sketch the skyline of a city near the top of the paper as shown. Outline the skyline in black. Add some windows near the top of the buildings if desired.

❺ Color flames above the rooftops.

❻ Write about Mose's life during each of the age periods shown in the pictures. You may wish students to write directly on the construction paper or on pieces of writing paper cut to size and then glued in the appropriate sections.

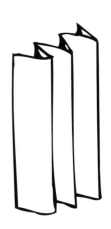

**Mose
the Firefighter**

Mose
Grows Up

age _____

age _____

age _____

age _____

age _____

Literature Pockets—Tall Tales • EMC 2732

Name: _____

A Proclamation of Honor

We the people of the great City of New York, do hereby honor the heroic efforts of Mose the Firefighter, who performed the following brave, selfless deeds:

_____

_____

_____

_____

_____

_____

To show our appreciation, we the people of New York City do hereby proclaim that

_____

_____

_____

_____

_____

_____

Signed,
The City of New York

How to Put Out a Volcano

Materials

- page 91, reproduced for each student (have extra copies available)
- 9" x 12" (23 x 30.5 cm) sheets of brown construction paper, two for each student
- scissors
- black marking pens
- 4" (10 cm) strips of red, yellow, and orange tissue paper
- glue
- stapler

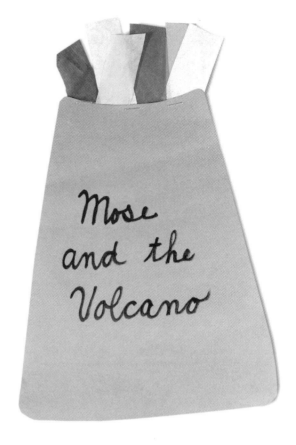

Steps to Follow

❶ Explain to students that they are to use their imagination to write how Mose put out the fire in a volcano. This may be written in the form of a story or as a list of directions for other firefighters.

❷ Guide students through the following steps to make a volcano-shaped product:

a. Write your story or directions on the volcano-shaped writing form. (You may use more than one form.)

b. Cut out the form. Trace it on two sheets of brown construction paper and then cut out the two volcano-shaped pieces—one for the front cover of your story and one for the back.

c. Use a black marking pen to write a title on the front cover. Glue strips of red, yellow, and orange tissue paper to the top of the cover to represent fire and lava.

d. Staple your story or directions between the front and back covers. You may staple along the top, bottom, or left side of the sheets.

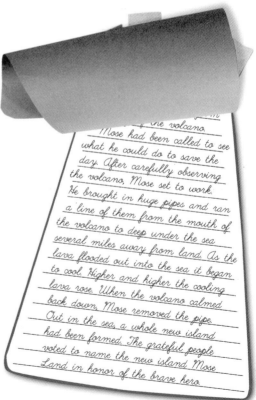

Volcano Writing Form

_____

_____

_____

_____

_____

_____

_____

_____

_____

_____

_____

_____

_____

_____

_____

Write an Original Tall Tale

Note: Have students complete this activity and the forms on pages 93 and 94 to create a pocket that contains their own tall tale.

Materials
- 8½" x 11" (21.5 x 28 cm) writing paper
- 9" x 12" (23 x 30.5 cm) construction paper
- crayons, colored pencils, marking pens
- stapler

Steps to Follow

❶ In advance, write the outline at right on the chalkboard or on chart paper.

❷ Review the elements of a tall tale with students. Refer to the tall tales already read. Remind students that a tall tale is a humorous story in which realistic details have been exaggerated to the point of being unbelievable. For example:

> **Realistic:** *Joey hit the baseball over the fence and scored a home run.*
>
> **Exaggerated:** *Joey hit the baseball so hard it flew over the fence, up through the atmosphere, around the sun, and landed in China.*

❸ Use the outline to guide students through the prewriting process. Work as a class to brainstorm possible characters, settings, and plots. Suggest that students think of a real experience and then exaggerate it. After the discussion, have students copy and complete the outline for their own tall tale.

❹ Remind students to focus on content as they write the first draft of their tall tale. Have them work with a partner to read, revise, and proofread their story before writing a final draft.

❺ After students complete their tall tale, have them make a construction paper cover for it. The cover should include the title of the tall tale, the author's name (their name), and an illustration of the main character or a scene from the story.

❻ Provide time for students to read aloud their tall tales. Invite listeners to identify the realistic and exaggerated elements of the story.

> ### Tall Tale Outline
> **Main Character/Hero**
>   Name:
>   Description:
> **Setting**
>   Location:
>   Time:
> **Adventure**
>   Sequence of events:
>   Conclusion:

Note: Reproduce this form for students. They are to design a bookmark and a pocket label similar to those created for the other pockets in their Tall Tales book.

Title

_____

_____

_____

_____

_____

_____

_____

_____

_____

_____

_____

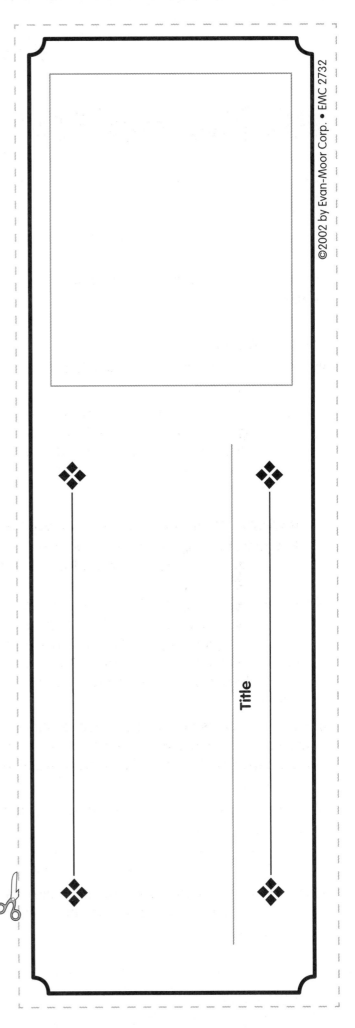

Title

Note: Reproduce this page for students. Have them complete the form using details from their own story to show that it has all the attributes of a tall tale.

Name: _____

Why Is It a Tall Tale?

_____
title

Attributes of a tall tale:	How the attribute was used in this story:
larger-than-life main character	
problem solved in a funny way	
exaggerated details	

Note: Use this evaluation activity after students have completed their Tall Tales book.

Name: _____

_____

title of tall tale

1. Who are the characters in this tall tale?

_____

_____

2. What is the setting of the story? (location and time)

_____

_____

3. What are the three most important events that happened in the tall tale?

_____

_____

_____

_____

4. I think this is a good example of a tall tale because _____

_____

_____

_____

_____

_____

_____

_____

Name: _____

Tall Tales

Read these attributes of a tall tale, and then give an example for each attribute from tall tales you have read.

• a larger-than-life main character

_____

_____

• a problem is solved in a funny way

_____

_____

• exaggerated details

_____

_____

Now write a definition for "tall tale."

_____

_____

_____

_____

_____

_____

_____

_____